UNIVERSE to GOD

The Ancient Wisdom of Sages
For Children

Anuradha Adarsh

WORK BOOK

Universe to God

by

Anuradha Adarsh

BLUEROSE PUBLISHERS

India | U.K.

Copyright © Anuradha Adarsh 2023

All rights reserved by author. No part of this publication may be reproduced, stored in a retrieval system or transmitted in any form or by any means, electronic, mechanical, photocopying, recording or otherwise, without the prior permission of the author. Although every precaution has been taken to verify the accuracy of the information contained herein, the publisher assumes no responsibility for any errors or omissions. No liability is assumed for damages that may result from the use of information contained within.

BlueRose Publishers takes no responsibility for any damages, losses, or liabilities that may arise from the use or misuse of the information, products, or services provided in this publication.

For permissions requests or inquiries regarding this publication,
please contact:
BLUEROSE PUBLISHERS
www.BlueRoseONE.com
info@bluerosepublishers.com

+91 8882 898 898

+4407342408967

ISBN: 978-93-5819-804-1

Cover design: Muskan Sachdeva

Typesetting: Rohit

First Edition: December 2023

"Our children are the gifts
Given by the mercy of the Lord.
They are delicate,
Take care of them
With love and devotion,
By imparting upon them
The ancient wisdom of sages."

CONTENTS

Preface   v

Wisdom Pages   Chapters

1	Wisdom Page 1	About	Universe	1
2	Wisdom Page 2	About	Om	3
3	Wisdom Page 3	About	Om Ma Ni Pad Me Hum	5
4	Wisdom Page 4	About	Gayathri Mantra	7
5	Wisdom Page 5	About	Flower of Life	9
6	Wisdom Page 6	About	Chakra Healing	11
7	Wisdom Page 7	About	God Page	13
8	Wisdom Page 8	About	Prayer	15
9	Wisdom Page 9	About	Mahavakyas	17
10	Wisdom Page 10	About	All Wisdom Pages	19
11			Prayer	21
12	Wisdom Page 3A		Prince to God	23
13	Wisdom Page 4A		King To Brahmarshi	27
14	Wisdom Page 9A		Aham Brahmasmi	31
15			Namaste	33
16			Gallery	35

Preface

What is Ancient Education, and what happened to it?

The Gurukul system of Indian education, derived from the ancient scriptures, was scientifically and spiritually conceived to provide a balance between human beings and society. This helped India prosper, and its people were known to be happy and civilized. However, with the passage of time and the arrival of foreign rulers, the wealth of knowledge was exploited for their own gains, resulting in the destruction or loss of invaluable teachings.

Why Ancient Wisdom Of Sages (AWS)?

These life lessons have been passed down through the ages via 'Shruti' or verbal communication by the ancient sages. The practices of meditation, yoga, chanting of the OM sound, and the realization of the existence of God or a supreme power have brought numerous benefits to humanity. Today's children need to understand their roots and acquire wisdom through this simplified, activity-based, and enjoyable form of education. Emphasis is placed on instilling good habits, character formation, and concentration in their pursuits.

In the present era, our children are the youth of tomorrow. It is essential for them to understand their origins and gain wisdom through an education system that is simplified, activity-based, and enjoyable. The development of good habits begins at an early age. We focus on building character, developing personalities, and teaching life lessons. This enables us to nurture individuals of exceptional character, bringing pride to humanity and fostering happiness and peace.

Vision
Our vision is to disseminate the correct knowledge of the ancient wisdom of the sages (our Vedas and Upanishads) worldwide, for the peace and happiness of every human being.

Mission

Spread awareness of ancient scriptures to children through online and offline workshops.
Implement a compulsory curriculum from UKG to PG that focuses on character development in children.
Conduct workshops for parents, highlighting the importance of early exposure to scriptures.
Publish books, workbooks, and online content through web-based platforms to further our cause.

Anuradha Adarsh

About Universe

Ancient Wisdom of the Sages
for Children
It gives us correct knowledge

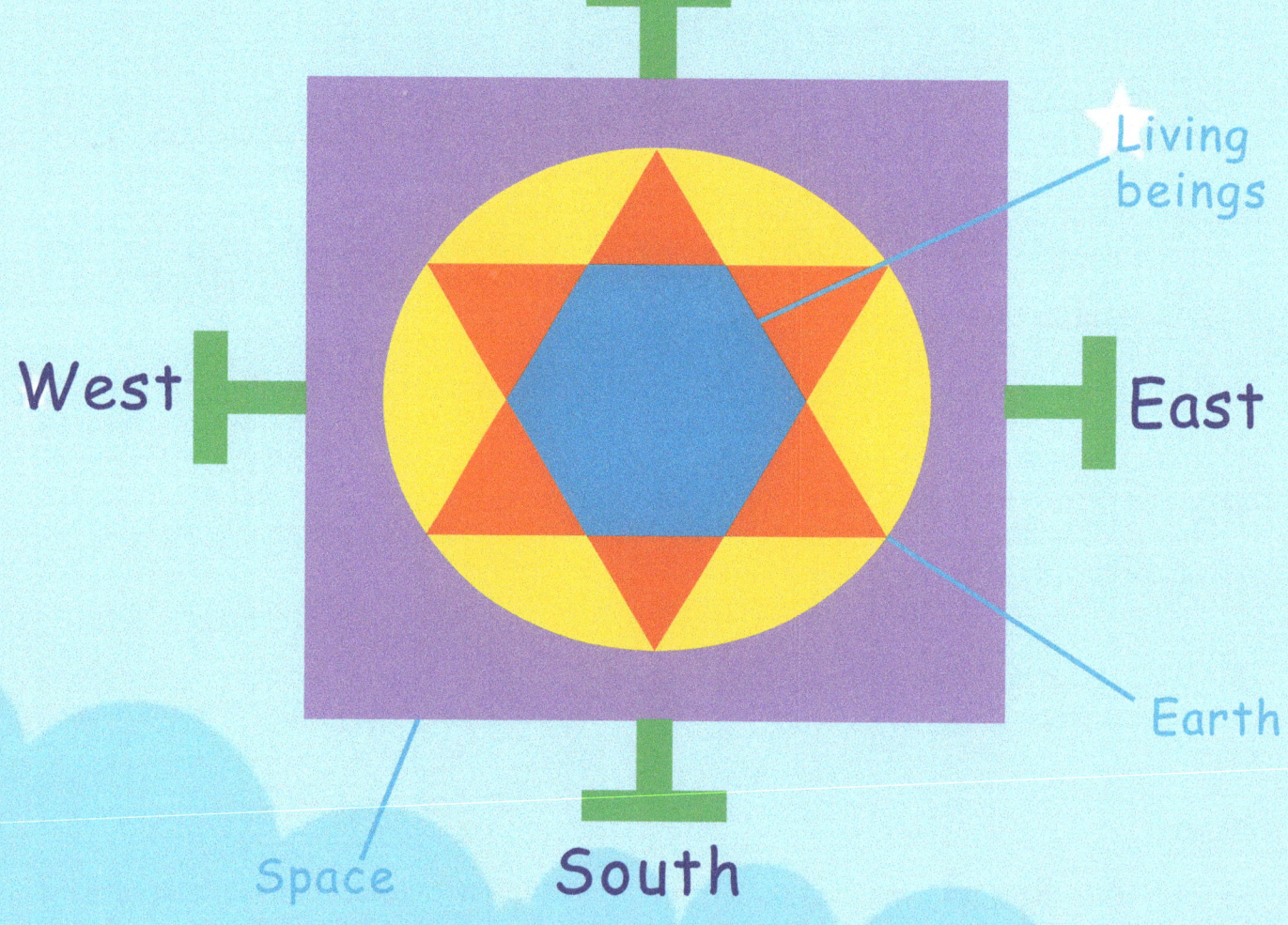

Symbol of Ancient Wisdom

From-Rigveda

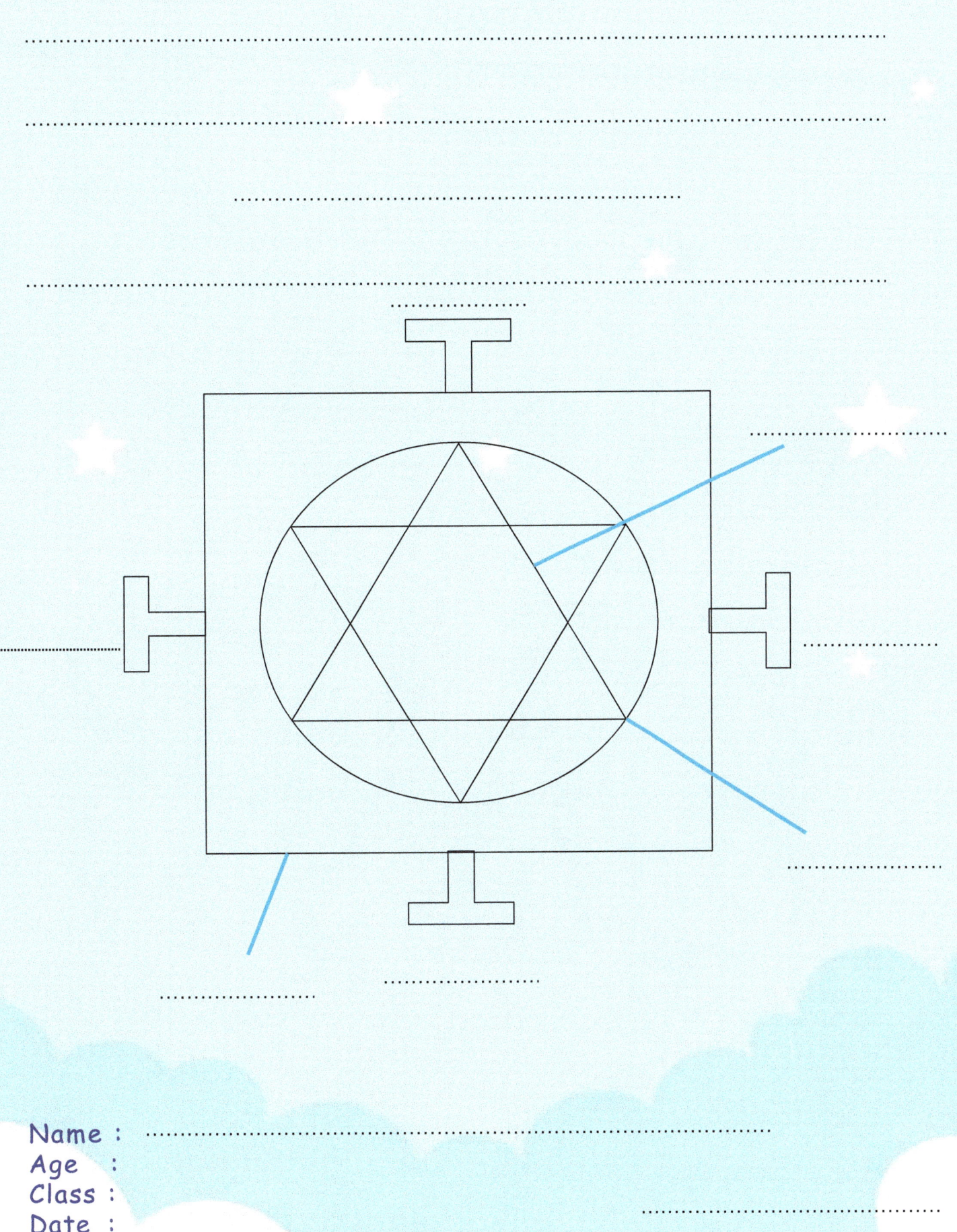

Name : ....
Age :
Class :
Date : ....

About Om

Wisdom Page 2

Om is the First Sound of the Universe
It Gives Concentration

Writing

Chanting

Listening

PatanjaliYogaSutra

Children will copy the work given on the left side of the book to the right side. 3

Name :
Age :
Class :
Date :

About Affirmation

I am	Om	Generosity
I am	Ma	Ethics
I am	Ni	Patience
I am	Pad	Perseverance
I am	Me	Concentration
I am	Hum	Wisdom

By Lord Buddha
Born in 535 BCE
Got enlightment in 7 Years

Children will copy the work given on the left side of the book to the right side.

....

....

....

....

....

Name :
Age :
Class :
Date :

Wisdom Page 4

Gayatri Mantra

Om bhur bhuvaha svaha
Tat savitur varenyam
Bhargo devasya dhimahi
Dhiyo yo nah prachodayat

ॐ भूर् भुवः स्वः।

तत् सवितुर्वरेण्यं।

भर्गो देवस्य धीमहि।

धियो यो नः प्रचोदयात् ॥

Writtenby
VishvaMitra
Rigveda 3.62.10{11}

Children will copy the work given on the left side of the book to the right side.

Name :
Age :
Class :
Date :

Flower Of Life

Wisdom Page 5

- It is Sacred Geometry
- It is The Cycle of Creation
- It is The Symbol of a Major Religions
- It Is 6000 Years Old
- It is found in the Whole Universe
- All Living things is according to its Sacred Ratio

Children will copy the work given on the left side of the book to the right side.

....

....

....

....

....

....

Name :
Age   :
Class :
Date :

7 Chakras

7 Minute Chakra Healing

Rigveda

Children will copy the work given on the left side of the book to the right side.

Name :
Age   :
Class :
Date :

12

About God

Supreme Divine Knowledge
Supreme Divine Power
Known As
"Brahman or God"

God has many names Brahma, Vishnu, Shiva, Rama, Krishna and More

Brahaman Created the Universe, the Sound OM, the Solar System, the Objects in Space & all living things

Brahman created 4 Scriptures for Human Beings which gives us Correct Knowledge of the whole World, Character Building & Personality Development.

RigVeda and VishnuPuran

Children will copy the work given on the left side of the book to the right side.

Name :
Age :
Class :
Date :

About Prayer

Oh God, Give Me Strength

I Will Do all my work with Pure, Peace and Truth

Pure   Peace   Truth

Isha-Upanishad

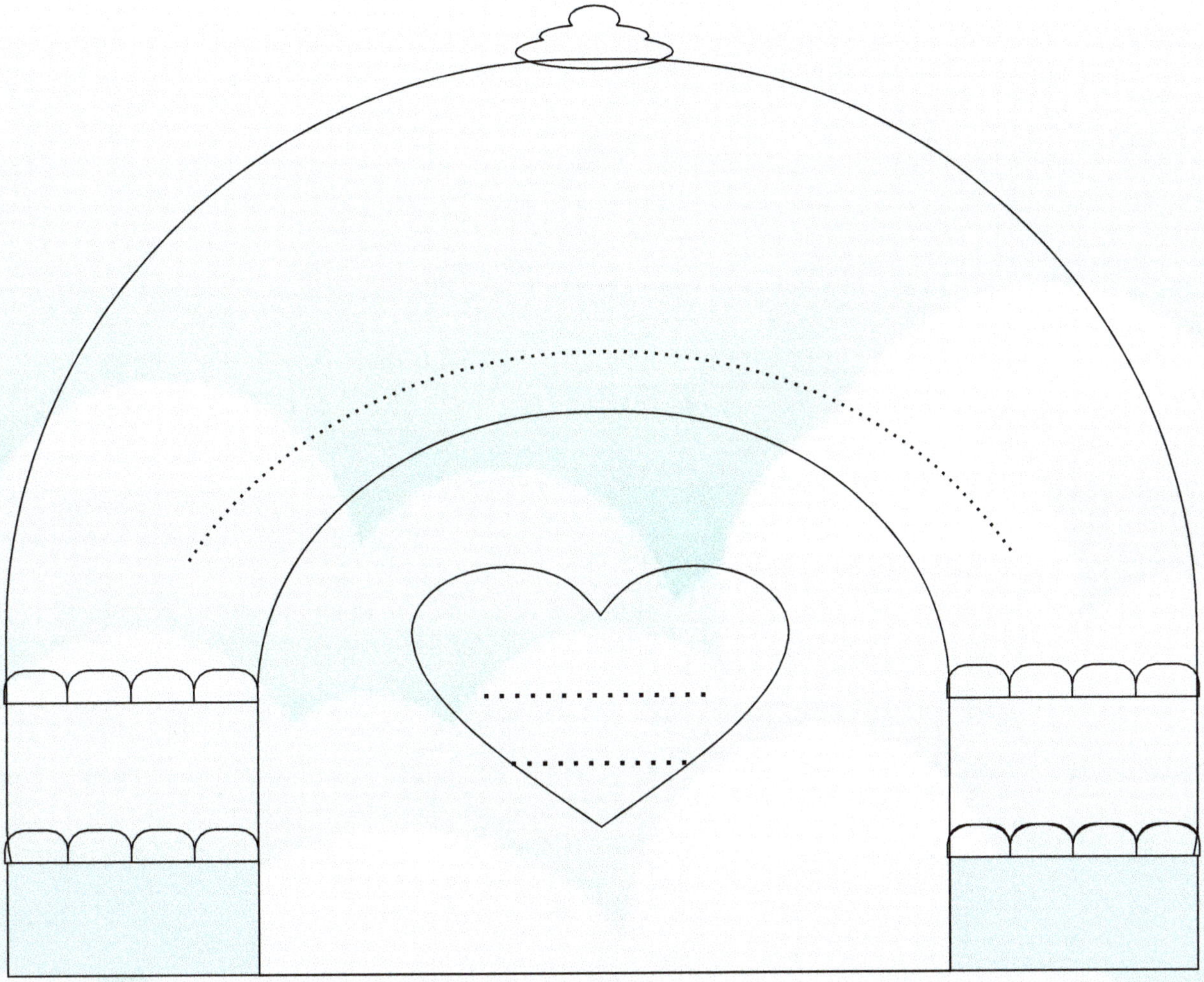

....

....

....

....

....

ॐ
....

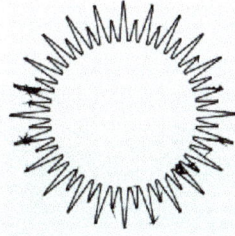
....

....

Name :
Age :
Class :
Date :

Mahavakyas

- Brahman is Real
  World is Unreal
- Brahman is Supreme
  Divine Knowledge
- Brahman is one without a second
- Brahman and Atman is one
- We are Brahman

अहम् ब्रह्मास्मि

अहम् ब्रह्मास्मि

अहम् ब्रह्मास्मि

Yajur Veda

Name :
Age   :
Class :
Date :

About All Wisdom Pages

Wisdom Page -1 About the Universe	**Wisdom Page -2** Om is the First Sound Of the Universe	**Wisdom Page-3** Om Ma Ni Pad Me Hum Affirmation
Wisdom Page-4 Gayatri Mantra Origin & Meaning	**Wisdom Page-5** Flower of Life Sacred Geometry	**Wisdom Page -6** 7 Chakras Chakra Healing
Wisdom Page-7 God Page Supreme Divine Power & Knowledge	**Wisdom Page -8** Prayer Page I am a Shrine Of Lord God is in me	**Wisdom Page -9** Mahavakyas अहम् ब्रह्मास्मि

Children will copy the work given on the left side of the book to the right side.

Name :
Age :
Class :
Date :

20

Our Prayer
I am a shrine of Lord - God is in me

I Am		I Am
PEACE		PEACE
PURE		PURE
TRUE		TRUE

My self
I am a shrine of Lord - God is in me
I am peace pure and truth
Aham Brahmasmi
Aham Brahmasmi
Aham Brahmasmi

Thanks to God
Thank you, God. You made a beautiful universe for us.
Thank you, God. For creating the earth for us to live on.
Thank you, God. You made scriptures, which gives knowledge of the whole universe

Prayer to God
Oh God give me the strength. I do all my work with

Peace, pure and truth.
Oh God, I receive correct knowledge from all directions.
Oh God, I receive noble thoughts from all directions.
Oh God, guide me to the right goal for my life.
Oh God I live happily with my family...

Children will copy the work given on the left side of the book to the right side.

Prince To God

A Story of Kindness

Once upon a time, there was a kingdom named Kapilavasthu, ruled by a king named Suddhodana. The king was blessed with a beautiful baby boy named Siddhartha.

After the birth of a baby boy, King Rajpurohit said this boy has a very bright future. He will become a very famous king. He will give birth to a new religion, or Dharma, and spread this dharma in the whole world, and the world will call him God.

Siddhartha was a bright, happy, kind, and gentle child.

The prince grew up and married a beautiful princess, Yashodhara. But Siddhartha was unhappy at the palace.

Children will copy the work given on the left side of the book to the right side.

....

....

....
....
....
....
....
....
....
....
....
....
....
....

Name :
Age :
Class :
Date :

One day, he told his servant Channa, "Let's go for a ride outside the palace." The prince saw a man bent with age.
A sick man who was crying in agony and a dead body was being carried by a group of people.
The king then asked Channa, "What is this?"
Channa answered that every person who was born, grew up, and eventually died one day
The king was very upset. He left everything and went to the forest in search of answers.
Why do people get sick and die?
The King then visited Alara Kalama, a Guru, and many other Gurus in his quest to find the answers.
But he is not able to get the answer. What is happiness?
Then Siddhartha sat under a tree until he got the answer himself. And he spread the preaching to his disciples, and then people called him Gautam Buddha. Then Gautam Buddha's teachings became dharma known as Buddha dharma.
And Buddha Dharam spread to many countries.
His teachings were very simple; people could learn them easily. After a while, everyone called him God.
That's why a kind prince became a god.

His four noble truths are:
1. Life is full of suffering.
2. Suffering is caused by desire.
3. Humans can free themselves from all that.
4. Truth be told, the way to achieve this freedom

And eightfold path;
The steps of the Noble Eightfold Path are
1. Right understanding,
2. Right Thought
3. Right speech
4. Right Action
5. Right Livelihood
6. Right Effort
7. Right mindfulness
8. Right Concentration

Children will copy the work given on the left side of the book to the right side.

Name :
Age :
Class :
Date :

King to Brahmarishi

Story of - Greed, Anger, Ego, jealous & Comparison

Thousands of years ago there was once a kind and generous king named Kaushik who was touring his kingdom. Near the end of his tour he came across an ashram lead by Vashisht Rishi. He and his army were invited to have a meal at the ashram, the rishi called a cow named Nandini who made many delicious dishes for them

Greed:
Here he had greed, the king wanted the cow for himself so he asked politely but he was refused.

....
....
....
....
....
....
....
....
....
....

Name :
Age :
Class :
Date :

Anger:
Here he had Anger, so he used force but he was unable to take Nandini since she was god's cow.

He thought '*Is spiritual power stronger than Physical power?*' He went and prayed to Shiva and received power stronger than physical powers of air, water, and fire and tried to defeat the rishi.

EGO:
Here he had EGO, after a long fight he lost, so he went and prayed to Brahma.

Jealousy :
Here he had Jealousy, he wished to be a rishi which was granted. He still couldn't defeat the rishi.

Comparison:
Here he had Comparison, so he prayed to Vishnu and asked to be a Brahmarishi.

Now he lost all his greed, anger ego, jealousy and comparison and didn't want Nandini anymore. He became a Brahmarishi, God gave him revelation which came out of his mouth as Gayatri Mantra. Since then he is known as Vishwamitra.

Gayatri Mantra

Om bhur bhuvaha svaha
Tat savitur varenyam
Bhargo devasya dhimahi
Dhiyo yo nah prachodayat

ॐ भूर् भुवः स्वः।
तत् सवितुर्वरेण्यं।
भर्गो देवस्य धीमहि।
धियो यो नः प्रचोदयात् ॥

Children will copy the work given on the left side of the book to the right side.

Name :
Age :
Class :
Date :

Aham Brahmasmi

Atman

Supreme Divine Knowledge
Supreme Divine Immortal Power
who made and control the
Universe including Us is
Brahman

We

AUM is the bow; Atman is the arrow.
Brahman is the target;
Aim precisely such that the arrow
Become merged with the target.

Anuradha Adarsh

Yajurveda
Mundaka Upanishad
Canto 2 - Verse 4

Children will copy the work given on the left side of the book to the right side.

Name :
Age :
Class :
Date :

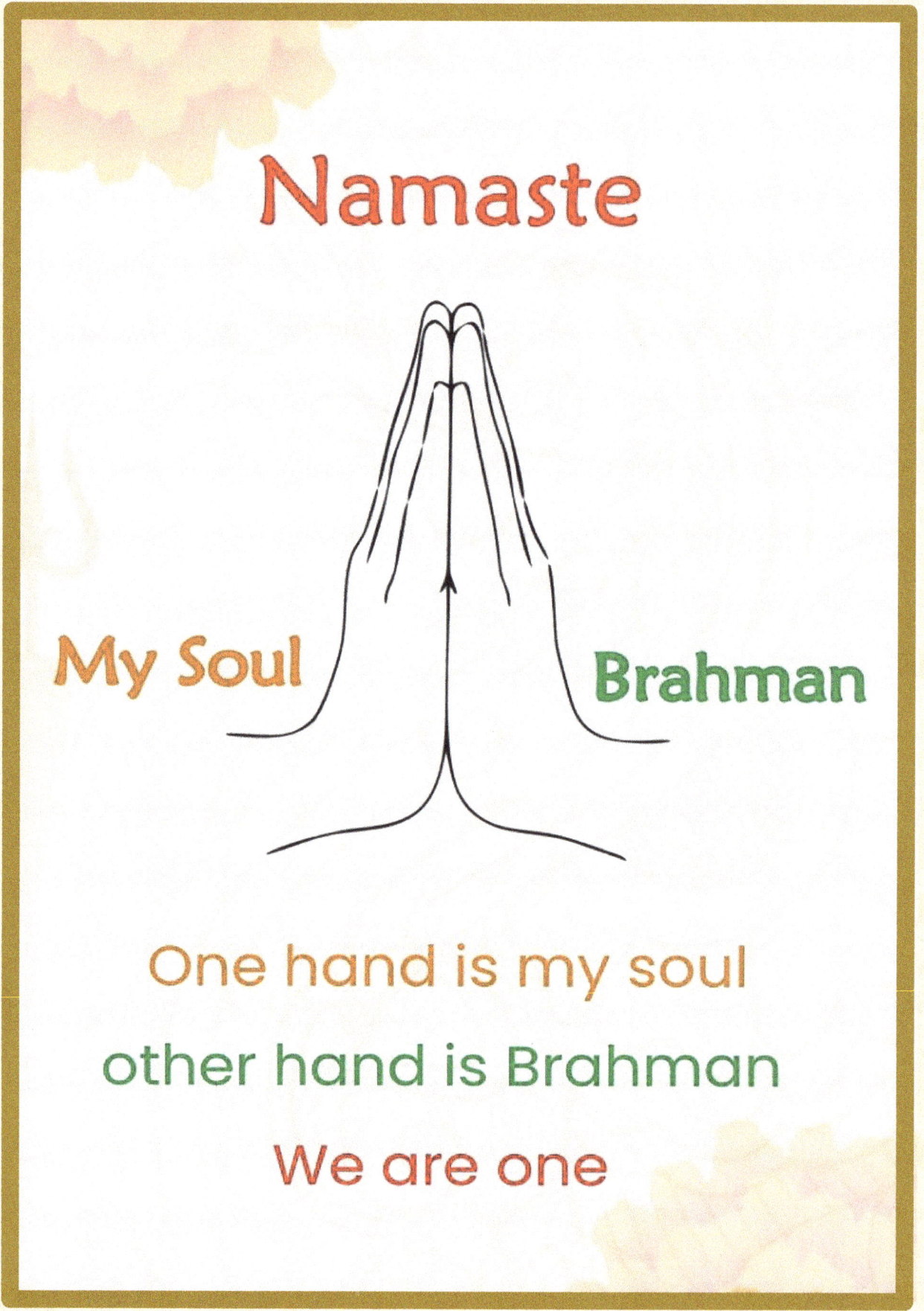

Children will copy the work given on the left side of the book to the right side.

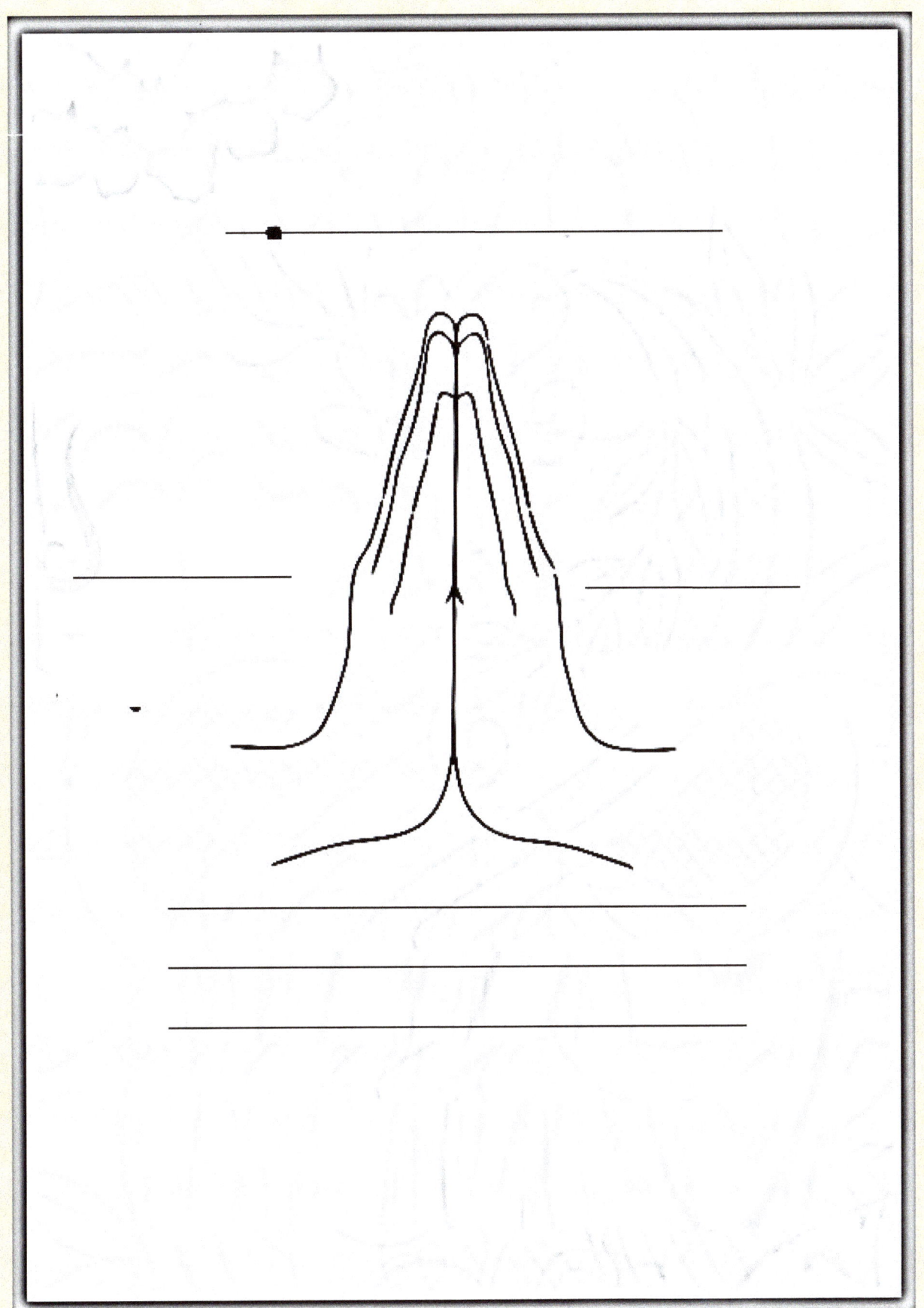

Children Are Saying About The Author

Anuradha Aunty

You are kind, sweet and generous. You are very good at teaching. You helped me and you made, made me at the top of the class. You are a good person. You are so nice. And because of you, I have more creativity, knowledge and kindness. Thanks to you, I have so many things to learn and teach. You are funny and taught me the most from all teachers that have taught me. So, from me to you - Thank you from the bottom of my heart. ♥

From - Reva
To - ♥ Aunty.

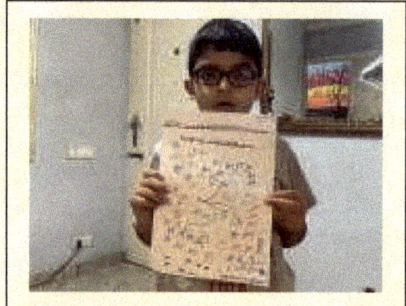

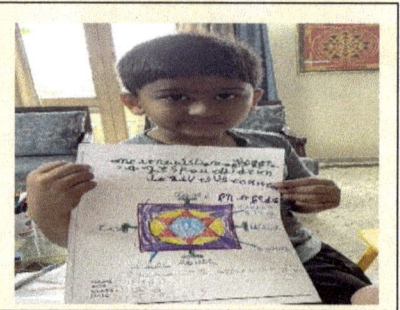

www.ingramcontent.com/pod-product-compliance
Lightning Source LLC
LaVergne TN
LVHW070535070526
838199LV00075B/6785